Wherever the road...
A journey of self-discovery in the second year after the loss of my love

Becky Gibler

ALSO BY BECKY GIBLER:

Borne of Grief and Flow: A journey of grief and healing after the loss of my love.

Wherever The Road…
A journey of self-discovery in the second year after the loss of my love.

© 2023 Becky Gibler

All rights reserved. No part of this publication may be reproduced, distributed, or transmitted in any form or by any means, including photocopying, recording, or other electronic or mechanical methods, without the prior written permission of the author, except in the case of brief quotations embodied in critical reviews and certain other noncommercial uses permitted by copyright law.

ISBN: 979-8-35092-678-1

Acknowledgements

As I sat down to make a list of people I wanted to thank, I wrote down several names of those who have helped with this book in some fashion, but there are many more who have supported me on my grief and healing journey, and I want to also acknowledge them here. I was thinking of this chapter of my life as the "Solo Becky Project," but I am reminded once again that this is a journey we do not take alone.

Most of you knew Pam, which means you also lost someone dear to you. In my early grief, I wasn't able to acknowledge that enough. I can now, and I appreciate all of you who were able to grieve and offer support at the same time.

First and foremost, I would like to thank my wonderful son, Spencer Haddenham-Gibler. He and I have walked this path together, and I like to think we have supported each other, but in those early months of grief, he was the only reason I got out of bed each morning. Spencer, you are the light of my life and the best son a mother could ever hope for. I am so proud of you, and I know Pam is watching over you with love and pride. I love you very much!

To my parents, Steve and Linda Gibler, thank you for your love and support and for not trying to talk me out of a solo road trip. I know I caused you anxiety and many gray hairs along the way, and I'm sure there were times when you wished I was already home safely, but I ended up with some pretty good stories (and great lessons), didn't I? Oh, yeah – and this book!

To my brother, sister-in-law, and niece, Frank, Sheila, and Maddy Gibler, thanks for listening to me and sharing stories of Pam, even though I know I repeated the same ones over and over. Frank, thanks for thinking ahead and sending me off with a gift that became very important on my road trip. The readers will have to keep reading to find out what that was!

Jess Chandler and Chris Laine, thank you for the daily check-ins, encouragement, love and support. You accepted my pain and sadness and allowed me to feel whatever came up in the moment. You helped me find ways to honor Pam ("Pam Points!"), which gave me purpose in those early months. Thanks for letting me stay with you on my road trip and for showing me some beautiful places I have never seen before. Your friendship is priceless.

Kelly and Jode Haddenham-Roe, where do I even start? You stepped in right away with things I didn't know I needed - Costco trips, dinner invitations, and so much more (BSB!). You offered a shoulder to cry on without judgement. Thank you for the beautiful wind chime that continues to remind me of Pam.

Wendi Sargent, your gentle counseling style was exactly what I needed when I was in my deepest grief. You helped me remember that relationships are about the entire time together and not just the last moments. The idea and title for my first book came from one of our sessions, and I am grateful for your feedback on both books.

Cynthia Grace and Kelly Damman, I met you both after Pam died and will be forever grateful for your friendship and our unfiltered conversations. You two are never afraid to tell me when you think I am a "hot mess!" Sometimes denial is a good thing, but other times, we need our friends to point out reality and help guide us down the right path. I love you both!

Coach Debby Handrich, what can I say but thank you for changing the trajectory of my life in February 2022. Without your guidance, this road trip may have never come to fruition, and my first book would still be sitting in a folder on my computer, unshared. Through my grief, you heard my desire for possibilities, freedom, and choices, and you gently led me to the trailhead where I could embark on the journey to find what I needed.

Jacob Peltier, I could not have asked for a more supportive friend and boss. You checked in daily and were so very patient with my grieving process. "Zoom Happy Hour" was a great invention! I appreciate your willingness to work with me when I was struggling and to grant the much-needed time off for me to deal with the grief.

Rick Jenkins, you are another dear friend who continues to check in often. I loved getting your texts on the road asking, "Where in the world is Becky today?" You always find a way to make me laugh, and I appreciate you very much.

Becca Katz, thank you for taking the time to edit my manuscript and offer great advice. This book is better because of you and your honest feedback. We met right after my road trip, and it was such a joy to tell you about it and relive the experience. Thank you for putting a smile on my face! Our marathon conversations about, well everything, have been a blessing!

Brandon Mead, you have done so much to promote my book, and I appreciate you very much. From your first email, you have been encouraging, supportive, and so much more than you can ever know. You called me an author when I felt like an imposter, and you gave me the courage to continue sharing my story. Every time I removed something from my book because I felt too vulnerable, I thought of you and put it back in.

Carrie Goddard and Mary Lane, I am so glad I went to that campfire, and I'm grateful that we met on my road trip! You showed me that some strangers are just friends waiting to connect, and you taught me to trust in a way I hadn't been able to for a while. I loved sending you photos of my journey after we parted in Utah, and the conversations we have had since then have brought me much happiness.

Kim Brewster, I appreciated that you saw I needed some connection, and you allowed me to bombard you with the photos from my trip. I chose the best-of-the-best to show you, and those are the ones that ended up in the book. By the time this book is published, I hope we will have made another journey to Rocky Mountain National Park. I love you, Cuz!

Paula Russell and Linda Taylor, I didn't know you well before Pam died, but you have become the best of friends. We have had some great adventures together in the last three years, haven't we? Thank you for your continued kindness and for giving me a place to stay on those nights when I didn't want to be home in an empty house.

Lisa Wendel, your friendship means the world to me. I appreciate the great conversations we have about grief, healing, and life in general, but I also appreciate who you are as a person. You are one of the kindest and most thoughtful people I know, and I always find myself grounded after a visit with you. Thank you for being you.

Michele Howell, we have been on a similar path for the past three years, and I'm not sure where I would be today without your friendship and support. You allowed me to experience my raw emotions without judging me or trying to stop me from crying, and you were the first one to help me realize I want to support others who are grieving. Thank you, my friend! (((HUGS)))

Brooke Zimmers, you spent time with Pam in the hospital, and although I know you loved Pam and did that for her, you also allowed me to recharge, so I could better support her in her last few weeks. Thank you also for being there for me after Pam died and for taking on the hard task of cleaning out her office.

DuValle Daniel, thank you for sitting with me and sharing stories of Pam. Your presence helped more than you know, and I am so grateful to you.

To Pam's cousins who immediately let Spencer and me know we are still part of the family, thank you. I appreciate the cards, the gifts, the texts, and being included in family events. I know Pam would be very touched by your actions.

To all of Pam's friends and colleagues who rallied around Spencer and me, I am so grateful. You brought us meals, checked in on us, visited, and shared stories of Pam. You did this to honor Pam, and it absolutely warmed my heart. It meant so much to me to see how loved she was by all of you.

Although I have named many in this section, there are so many more who supported me in ways that I will never forget. Thank you to the ones who weren't afraid to give me a much-needed hug, even though it was the beginning of the pandemic. I was touched by the texts, phone calls, cards, and offers to help with yardwork, shopping, and anything else I needed. Thank you to everyone who showed up to the book launch for *Borne of Grief and Flow.*

If I forgot anyone, please know it was purely a lapse in memory and not intentional.

Praise for Wherever The Road...

Author Becky Gibler doesn't shy away from telling her personal story to help others heal. In her first book *Borne of Grief and Flow*, she brought readers along as she navigated the Pacific Northwest without her partner for the first time in nineteen years. Continuing the journey via thoughtful prose and breathtaking photography, in this highly anticipated follow-up, Becky hits the road and plants readers firmly in her passenger seat.

Traveling the country solo for two months, she tells her story utilizing her keen eye for the perfect shot. Beautiful stills of landscapes, historical landmarks, and up-close encounters with wild animals punctuate each stop on her trip. While documenting her adventures state-to-state in every color palette and form of weather, Becky proves that sometimes the thing you find while you think you're looking for a moose is actually the depth of your own resilience.

Persisting through the second year of her expedition through grief, she expertly uses her insightful words to guide readers through survivor's guilt and what it means to have fun again. To not just give yourself permission to let joy happen, but actively seek it. To pack up the car and see what the world still has to show you. To let new surroundings help you find the courage to accept a hug from a stranger. Soar through a blue sky. Take that road, even if you're not completely sure where it leads.

Becky demonstrates there is no limit to what shaking up our routine can teach us about ourselves, if we're willing to accept the call to adventure. *Wherever The Road...* is a remarkable addition to this series and must-read for anyone asking, "What now?" If you're seeking your next step after losing a loved one, or know someone who is, this book is for you.

—Brandon Mead, Event Host and Book Buyer, Third Place Books

Grief is very often referred to as a journey, which doesn't quite capture the messy, scary, erratic, and lonely nature of individual grief after a significant loss. This book beautifully catalogues two months through Becky's eyes and words, and captures the way one person faced her fears, gathered her courage, and took to the open road in search of, in her own words, "possibilities, freedom, and choices." What she found was so much more, and what she offers to anyone who opens this book is beauty, encouragement, and hope.

—Wendi Sargent, LMHC, Grief Counselor

Wherever The Road... is one woman's declaration to follow a calling into a bright, unchartered future. While her first book captured vulnerability and hope after the loss of her life partner, this second book shows Becky Gibler claiming a new identity. Each chapter highlights her creative and free experience as she let her camera chronicle a two-month road trip. The result? True healing that is rare, rewarding, and riveting!

—Debby Handrich, Spiritual Mentor, Writing Coach, and Hostess of Story U Talk Radio

This book is dedicated to those who saw the pain through my mask and knew I wasn't okay. Thank you for your love and support and for convincing me that I was worthy of self-care.

I started my journey, dubbed "The Solo Becky Project," with a heart full of grief. I thought I was doing okay, but I really wasn't. There I was, almost twenty months after the death of my partner, Pam, and I was still having trouble sleeping and focusing on day-to-day tasks; my full-time job seemed nearly impossible. Hell, on some days, just getting out of bed seemed impossible. Almost immediately after her death, I felt an overwhelming urge to get into the car and drive . . . anywhere. I didn't have a particular destination in mind, and I didn't know what I was looking for. No itinerary, no plans—I just wanted to drive. I wasn't sure if I was running away from something or toward something. I just knew that I *needed* to drive.

I suppose everything happens in its own time. I didn't get the chance to take that drive until twenty months into my journey of loss, grief, and learning, but it was the right time. Eight weeks later, I returned a different person, more resilient and more confident with the knowledge that I am capable of meeting life's challenges.

Grief is different for everyone, but there are common experiences among those who grieve. This is *my* story, yet I hope it resonates with many and inspires them to have the courage to go wherever the road may lead.

The first year of grieving the loss of a loved one is terrible. This is expected. You know all those "firsts" will be tough, and damn there are so many of them! The holidays, the birthdays, the anniversaries . . . even the day of the week and the date of the month on which your loved one died. Every Thursday and every ninth of the month were activators during the first year; they're still not easy, but they are much softer. The first anniversary of Pam's death was particularly emotional.

The second year of grief hit me with a vengeance—much like the initial loss, it can't be imagined; it can only be experienced. Instead of being able to remember what I was doing with Pam "last year," I felt only a vast emptiness upon realizing there will never again be another memory of what she and I were doing "last year." From there on, "this time last year" no longer existed for her, and for me, "this time last year" was a struggle to figure out my life without her in it. The memories essentially became a replay of my grief journey: this time last year was my first day without her; this time last year, I was writing her obituary; and on and on.

Pam died in July of 2020, so by December of 2021, I had grown used to the fact that there were no more memories of her from last year. Christmas of the second year was much easier than that of the first year, and I was learning to accept my new life. I thought I was doing okay, but grief can sneak up on you when you let your guard down and stop paying attention. Start getting a little too cocky, and grief will knock you on your ass. Sometime in early January of 2022, it hit me that I had entered *another full calendar* year without Pam. Grief is pure emotion. It can render an otherwise strong and intelligent person, weak and dazed. Dark thoughts entered my mind and slowly replaced the happiness that had been trying to take hold. My sleeping and eating habits regressed to those that I had during my early grieving days. It felt like all my progress was slowly fading away. Pam's unsettled estate weighed heavily on my mind. I was, once again, drowning in my grief. But I didn't understand why.

To move forward and try to live my best life, I began working with a life coach. She asked how I visualized my future and what I felt I needed to achieve it. While talking, three words emerged: possibilities, freedom, and choices. She could see that I was struggling with the grief again and strongly recommended that I take ninety days to "reset" my brain. With her encouragement, I spoke with my wonderfully supportive boss and arranged to take a three-month leave of absence.

On March 4, 2022, I packed up my car and headed out with only one plan—to leave town for a month and go wherever the road took me.

My first book, *Borne of Grief and Flow*, chronicled my first year of grief and healing through photography. I wrote it for people who are grieving to let them know that they are not alone and that the pain does get softer with time. I feel that healing from grief is a lifelong process. The challenges of life continue to ebb and flow, so although I felt good after I wrote the first book, it's no surprise that the grief hit again. The important thing for me was to embrace the grief, use the tools I had gathered along the way, and continue with the process of healing.

Wherever The Road... showcases some of the 10,000 photographs I took on this road trip; again, photography played a large part in my healing. In this book, I will share the lessons I learned on the road and how these lessons continue to help me heal and grow. While some lessons are specific to me and my situation, I hope my story resonates with others who are grieving and helps them move forward through the ups and downs.

Week 1

My journey began with a visit to my son in Portland, Oregon. We took a day trip to Cannon Beach, one of our favorite places. As I breathed in the sea air and listened to the waves crashing on the beach, I could feel Pam's presence. Back in Portland that night, I finally got to meet a new friend in person. We're in the same online "grief group," but since she lives in Florida, we had never met face-to-face. She was visiting a friend in Portland, so the three of us had dinner and went to enjoy some karaoke afterwards. Although I was determined to come out of my shell and take some chances on this trip, I was not quite ready to take the mic and sing! We took a selfie that I sent to two friends back home. They said I already looked different somehow—more relaxed, with a natural smile that they hadn't seen in a while.

After leaving Portland, I headed to Chiloquin and found a hotel for the night. I took the hour-long drive to the southern entrance of Crater Lake National Park; the temperature was low, and the snow was high. There were only a few other people there. I met a nice couple from New York, both Emergency Medical Technicians; we talked about the challenges they were facing during the pandemic. A man was cooking hot dogs on a camp stove. I almost asked if I could trade a few apples for a hot dog, but I didn't quite have the nerve. In another three weeks, when my confidence had increased, that question would have been easy to ask.

HAYSTACK ROCK,
CANNON BEACH, OREGON

CRATER LAKE NATIONAL PARK

From Crater Lake, I drove to Mt. Shasta, California. This was a sweet little town with beautiful lakes and stunning waterfalls. The cloud formations over the mountain were incredible.

Above: Hedge Creek Falls, Top right: near Crater Lake, Bottom right: a cloud formation in Mt. Shasta

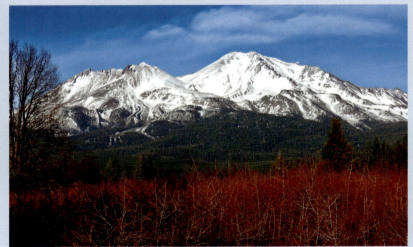

MT. SHASTA

Lesson One: Eating dinner alone in a restaurant won't kill you (although you may feel a little awkward at first).

If you ask a group of widows and widowers to list the top ten things that they find difficult to adjust to after the death of one's spouse, I bet you the vast majority will put "eating alone" on that list. This was one of the most difficult things for me to get used to after Pam died. It was hard enough to eat alone at home, but being alone in a restaurant was nearly impossible. I had only been out to eat once or twice by myself in the twenty months since she died, and it didn't feel right. On my first night in Mt. Shasta, I decided not to spend my entire road trip eating meals in hotel rooms. I went to a small Mexican restaurant across the street from my hotel and had the first of many dining out experiences on my trip. The host looked at me a little strangely and sat me back by the kitchen (a perplexing phenomenon that would continue throughout the next eight weeks). It could have been my imagination, but it seemed that all the employees looked at me with pity. I was called "Sweetie" no less than four times. I probably did look a little worn out and sad. Like I said, I was a different person when I returned from my journey, but you know what? I got through that dinner, and nothing bad happened. I did end up eating at the hotel the next night, though. Small steps, right?!

For the next three nights, I was able to find places to stay in Minden and Beatty, Nevada, and Quartzsite, Arizona. No plans, no reservations. I drove into town in my dark red Hyundai Tucson that I had affectionately named "Voyager" and hoped for something decent. Even when the accommodations were just so-so, the hospitality was wonderful, and I'm grateful to the friendly folks who recommended interesting sites that were off the beaten path and excellent local restaurants I would not have otherwise found.

There were days when I drove up to one hundred miles without seeing another car on the road. Eagles and hawks flew so close to my car that I could see the patterns on their feathers. This happened almost every day throughout the trip, and it brought a smile to my face and peace to my heart. I like to think that Pam sent them to keep me company along my way.

Castle Lake

McArthur-Burney Falls Memorial State Park, California

Pretty scenery between Carson City and Beatty, Nevada

BIG DUNE RECREATION AREA, AMARGOSA VALLEY, NEVADA

Lesson Two: People are better than you think they are (but it's still okay to keep your guard up!).

Widows and widowers can be terribly vulnerable to those with ill intent, whether the intended harm is physical, emotional, or financial. The message to "be careful and not be overly trusting" is prevalent in grief groups, and it's a sensible one. Loneliness and the desire to connect with someone on a deep level can lead a grieving person to let their guard down. I had been on the road for only a short time, but I was so impressed with how friendly people were. Everywhere I went, people struck up conversations with me. This kind of thing always happened to Pam—she was super friendly and could light up a room just by walking through the door. People gravitated toward her, but not usually toward me. I always told her she was too trusting; she told me I was not trusting enough. Now, I found myself happily responding to the smiles and casual greetings. This was new and intriguing and was perhaps one of the most important lessons I learned on my trip—it's okay to open yourself to others, even total strangers. I realized that I had been missing human connection. Due to the pandemic, I was working from home. I saw family and friends during weekends, but I missed the normal day-to-day interaction. I came to appreciate and enjoy the little conversations in grocery stores, restaurants, and hotel lobbies. Twice, when I stopped to get gas, I chatted with the station attendant. When I went to pay for a much-needed cup of coffee, I got a big smile and a, "It's on me!" It's interesting how something so simple could make me feel so good. As a woman traveling alone, I was always aware of my surroundings and somewhat guarded, but this little introvert was starting to come out of her shell.

Week 2

I traveled to Green Valley, Arizona, where I stayed six nights with some dear friends. These friends used to live close by in Washington; Pam and I loved spending time with them, and although we talked often, I hadn't seen them in almost a year. We had a wonderful time reconnecting and exploring southern Arizona's beauty. I saw a Vermilion Flycatcher and a jackrabbit on my first night. When I ventured out another night, I saw a roadrunner and a coyote!

Daytime blue skies and the sun's warmth on my skin felt amazing and helped to boost my mood. I thought about visiting a few more friends and family on this trip but realized that I had a lot of healing ahead of me, and the only way I could really focus on my needs was to do the rest of the trip solo.

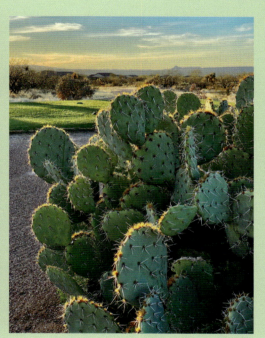

I headed off to New Mexico, a state I had never been to before. Maybe because this was uncharted territory for me, it was on this stretch of road that I truly started letting go of the stress and pain that had been building up since Pam died. I stayed in Silver City, where I visited with the locals in shops and restaurants, breathed in the fresh, warm air as I hiked up to the Gila Cliff Dwellings, and soaked up the silence at the City of Rocks. It was amazing, and although I missed Pam terribly, I felt her presence and realized I would be okay.

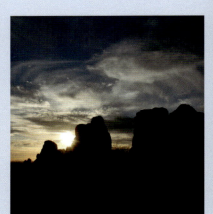

Lesson Three: Give yourself the freedom to be flexible and change your mind.

The ability to *change* your mind is a funny concept when you can't even make a simple decision in the first place. After Pam died, I temporarily lost the ability to make a decision—any decision. I'm amazed that I was able to dress myself each day! I also found that once I had finally decided something or made plans with someone, any deviation from that plan caused more stress. It felt like another loss and another thing over which I had no control.

While in Silver City, I decided to sign up for a volunteer shift at the Best Friends Animal Sanctuary in Kanab, Utah. My life coach told me about this place before I left Washington, but I had not yet been ready to make that commitment. After two weeks on the road, I decided this was something I wanted to do, so I formulated a plan and headed west again.

I must admit that a part of me was sad to deviate from the "no plan, no itinerary" scenario, but I reminded myself that this trip was about healing and resetting. What can be better for healing than volunteering with animals? And despite the deviation, I still followed the road wherever it took me, even when I probably shouldn't have . . .

WEEK 3

On the way to Kanab, Utah, I felt compelled to go to Sedona, Arizona. Pam and I had gone there many years ago, but for just a few hours. I decided to stay a couple of nights, stopping at Tonto Natural Bridge State Park along the way.

There's something very special about Sedona—as I drove into the city, I felt shielded from all my grief and sadness. I had good conversations with Navajo women who were selling pottery and jewelry along the roadside. I walked around the Uptown area and did some shopping. Even though it was hot and bustling with people, most seemed to be in a good mood and were friendly.

Tonto Natural Bridge State Park

A visit to the Chapel of the Holy Cross was more emotional than I had expected. I'm not Catholic, but the large crucifix on the wall and the reverent silence of tourists sitting in the pews touched me in an unanticipated way. The air was filled with a mixture of joy and sorrow. My gaze fell on the rows of candles to my right; I lit one for Pam and another for a friend's partner who had also passed.

Sedona is an International Dark Sky Community, and the airport is a popular spot to view the star-filled sky. I hiked near the airport during the day and returned later to take photos at sunset.

I would have liked to stay in Sedona longer, but I was due in Kanab in a few days, and there were things to see along the way.

Before leaving Sedona, I visited Red Rock State Park. I then went to the Grand Canyon on my way to Marble Canyon, my next stay. I had never been to the Grand Canyon before and hadn't realized how grand it actually is! If you need to be reminded of how small you are in the overall scheme of things, a visit to the Grand Canyon will do it. This wasn't a bad realization though—it was more of a feeling that many have come before, and many will follow; all we have is a little speck of time in between, and what we do with it is entirely up to us.

Red Rock State Park

GRAND CANYON

Lesson Four: Allow yourself to trust.

The death of a loved one completely changes your world from what you knew to be true just a moment earlier. It becomes hard to trust anything or anyone, and then it becomes hard to trust yourself, your instincts, and your abilities. The irregular sleeping and eating habits, depression, and memory loss just exacerbate these feelings.

Before I left on "The Solo Becky Project," I had two recurring visions. One was me feeling very small and looking up at big red rocks. That was a given if I was traveling in Arizona, Utah, or Nevada, but it was a specific image in my head that I had not yet come across in my travels. The other was me sitting around a campfire, meeting new friends. Well, any introvert can tell you that the odds of that happening are slim unless an extrovert is dragging you along. We introverts don't usually put ourselves out there or allow random strangers to become friends.

I had to tell myself over and over again to trust the process and allow things to happen the way they were meant to happen. For this journey to work, I had to trust other people; more importantly, I had to learn to trust myself again.

The first thing I did in Kanab was visit Zion National Park. As I entered the park, I was filled with a sense of wonder. It was one of the most beautiful places I had ever seen, and the peacefulness was even greater than what I had felt in Sedona. I spent several hours walking around taking photos. This is where I encountered the wall of big red rocks from my visions, and it was awe-inspiring!

Wall of red rocks in Zion National Park

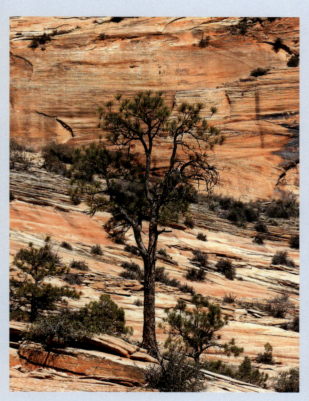

Zion National Park

As I was checking into the hotel later that day, the front desk attendant told me that there's a campfire every night on the hotel grounds. I didn't think much of it until later that night when it was time for the campfire to start. I almost didn't go—did I mention I'm an introvert?—but something told me I needed to be there, so I tentatively headed out. It was nice meeting the folks who had gathered, but I didn't feel any real connection with anyone until two women showed up a little later, and I just knew I was supposed to talk to them. I asked them where they got the ice cream that they were enjoying, and thus began an unexpected friendship. They were old college roommates who came together each year to volunteer at the animal sanctuary, so we started talking about that, and the easy conversation continued into the early morning hours. Up to this point of my trip, I hadn't told anyone about Pam, but it felt right to tell these women, and I showed them my first book. Confiding in them felt liberating, and it reinforced the lesson that I needed to learn to trust. We spent more time together over the next couple of days, and I sent them pictures of my journey as it progressed from there. I'm happy to say that we have become great friends and get together as often as we get the chance.

Volunteering at the sanctuary gave me a sense of purpose. I took an old dog named Raja out for half a day. We rode in the car and took several walks. It was fun to watch how excited he was to get out and about—kind of like how I was feeling myself! Later that day, I had lunch with my two new friends. This was the first meal I had eaten with someone since I left my friends in Arizona, and it felt nice.

Above: the campfire at the hotel
Left: Best Friends Animal Sanctuary in Angel Canyon
Right: Raja

The day after volunteering, I visited Kodachrome Basin State Park, Bryce Canyon National Park, and the Coral Pink Sand Dunes State Park. I continued to be blown away by the beauty all around me. The stillness and lack of people was mesmerizing and peaceful. A change in my mentality was taking place, and my soul was getting exactly what it needed.

Coral Pink Sand Dunes State Park

THOMPSON SPRINGS, UTAH AND BUTCH CASSIDY'S CHILDHOOD HOME IN CIRCLEVILLE, UTAH

WEEK 4

Of the nine states I visited, Utah was my favorite for photography and enjoying nature. After Kanab, I went to Moab, where I visited Arches National Park, Potash Dinosaur Tracks and Petroglyphs, Dead Horse Point State Park, and Canyonlands National Park. All were incredible, and I saw more of the big red rocks.

Moab is where I decided that one month was not going to be long enough for my road trip. It's also the place where lessons five and six came into play.

Arches National Park

POTASH ROAD

Dead Horse Point State Park

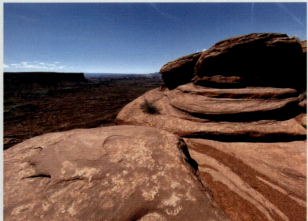

Canyonlands National Park

Lesson Five: Having fun is important (and is nothing to feel guilty about!).

I've heard so many people who have lost a loved one say that they can't be happy anymore or that they can't have fun because it feels wrong; it's like they are doing a disservice to their loved one just by laughing. Initially after Pam died, I was very sad, and it took almost a year to start being regularly happy again. But even in that first year, I didn't deny happy feelings when I felt them because Pam had always been so full of life and laughter.

Eventually, I realized that even though I was *allowing* myself to have fun when it presented itself, I wasn't *seeking* fun; there is a huge difference that I realized only when I picked up a flyer for a hot air balloon ride. Part of me felt guilty because I was supposed to be taking this time off to reflect on how I was feeling and to continue healing from my grief. Then I realized this trip was about working through the sadness, and what better way to do that than to have fun, smile, and laugh? Pam would have wanted nothing less for me and would be encouraging me to have fun if she were here.

I have wanted to go on a hot air balloon ride since I was a kid. I'm not sure why I waited so long, but on a brisk morning at the end of March, I got up early and headed out to the meeting site in Moab. Thirteen other passengers and I were loaded into two vans and driven to the airport to watch the crew inflate our balloon. I very clumsily hefted myself over the three-and-a-half-foot wall of the wicker basket and managed to land upright next to the pilot and gas tanks. Our balloon slowly and silently soared over Canyonlands National Park for about an hour before quickly gliding over the heads of some unsuspecting campers and landing in a dirt field. Our pilot poured champagne, and we all toasted the flight and safe landing. It was an amazing ride and well worth the wait.

Views of Canyonlands National Park from the hot air balloon.

Lesson Six: Fear is a state of mind.

Many who have lost a spouse talk about how scared they have become. For some, it's because their spouse made them feel safe; for others, it's just because they now live alone and feel more vulnerable. A common fear is that someone else we love will die soon. As mentioned earlier, the death of a spouse can often lead to memory loss, depression, and a loss of trust in yourself. You lose your sense of safety which allows fear to drive your decisions.

I am a strong and capable person with keen situational awareness. I almost always feel safe because I am prepared and cautious. I felt like it was my job to keep Pam safe and protected. But after she died, I became irrationally afraid of many things. I double- and triple-checked the door locks at night and then checked them again. I changed the locks in the house, installed a camera system, and added a lock to my bedroom door. Unexpected noises startled me, and I was always on edge. Nothing about my physical surroundings had changed, but my mental state was more fragile than ever before.

I have been very responsible and careful all my life. At times, I declined adventures because I felt like I needed to stay safe to take care of the ones I love. I was afraid to take chances and really *live*. When I allowed myself to get in that hot air balloon, I also gave myself permission to experience other opportunities.

The day after the balloon ride, I held in my hand another flyer that I had grabbed in the hotel lobby—for skydiving. I had never wanted to skydive; in fact, the thought had always terrified me. I'm still not sure why I took that flyer. For the first time in my life, I was intrigued with the idea. After all, this journey was about shaking up my brain and breaking free from the grief patterns and painful memories that I couldn't seem to get rid of. What better way of shaking things up than jumping out of a plane from a height of 13,000 feet? As I hesitated to dial the reservation line, I asked myself how I would feel if I left town without doing this. My answer was immediate and clear: I would be disappointed and upset with myself. I calmly placed the call and made the reservation for the next day.

I thought I wouldn't sleep the night before the jump, but I slept like a baby. The next morning, I drove to the same airport where the hot air balloon was launched. I put on the tandem jump harness, climbed into the airplane, and was strapped to Andrew, who would have my life in his hands for about six minutes. I was super excited and only a little nervous. Andrew was hilarious and made the whole experience very enjoyable. We were the first out of the plane and the last on the ground, so we had a good, long jump. It was the most exhilarating adventure of my life and gave me such a feeling of empowerment. As the wind took my breath away and the ground got closer, I was regaining more and more of my old confidence. After jumping out of the plane, I felt like I could do anything! The adrenaline "high" lasted for at least three days, and I was so proud of myself for conquering a life-long fear.

Photo credit: Skydive Moab

WEEK 5

From Moab, I drove to Salt Lake City and visited the Tracy Aviary. The next day, I left the warmth of Utah and arrived in Jackson, Wyoming, my first time in that state. I visited the National Elk Refuge and Grand Tetons National Park. On the second day in Jackson, it started snowing, and by the fourth day, there was a nice snow cover on the ground; I got up before sunrise to take pictures. I was incredibly grateful to see a large herd of elk, several moose, and some deer. The effect that Nature had on my soul is indescribable. It was a feeling that everything would turn out okay and that I could continue to move through the grief and survive. In the stillness of the peaceful morning, I could finally breathe again.

Driving on, I arrived in Gardiner, Montana, on day thirty-five. The weather was beautiful again, and I took a short walk from my hotel to the entrance of Yellowstone National Park. There were rumors of a grizzly having been sighted earlier that evening, so I planned to get up early the next morning to see if it came back. Apparently, it had been feasting on a bison carcass for three days. The next morning, as luck would have it, the grizzly was spotted again. I could tell by all the photographers lined up on the side of the road that I was in the right place. I barely had time to park and get my camera out before the bear quickly left the area—he was done feasting and left the rest of the kill for the black and white wolves that came soon after. It was exciting to get to see all that animal activity, especially the grizzly, and I'm glad I snapped a few quick shots before he ran away. Later, I drove further into the park, where I saw herds of bison and elk. What an amazing time!

THE ROOSEVELT ARCH AT YELLOWSTONE'S NORTH ENTRANCE.

WEEK 6

The next stop was Missoula for a few days. It was bitterly cold and windy, and it snowed off and on, so I took this time to just rest and relax without doing any sightseeing. This hotel also had a campfire each night, and I now found myself eager to meet new people. I ran into a firefighter from Portland, Oregon named John—I mean that literally—he was coming toward the door while I was going out, and we ran into each other! I told him I was checking to see if anyone was at the campfire, and we agreed to meet out there in a bit. It was still cold, but the wind had died down. We talked for a while, and I felt like I could trust him with my story. I told him about Pam, and he told me about his family. He taught himself to play the guitar during the pandemic, so he played and sang that night. It was a fun time. Before he went back inside, he asked if he could give me a hug, saying that he guessed I hadn't had many of them on my journey. He was right, and it felt nice to be hugged.

Lesson Seven: Always follow your intuition (but sometimes you learn great lessons if you don't).

Even in the absence of grief, it's not always easy to follow your intuition. Sometimes, your rational brain gets in the way, or a lack of information prevents you from making the best choice.

I'm usually great at following my intuition, but the ability has faltered since Pam died. My emotions were so raw for so long that I stopped being in tune with my gut instinct, which usually guided me in making sensible decisions and kept me out of trouble. Moving ahead, an impulsive move that could have led to disaster turned out to be a great lesson.

Before I started my trip, I arranged to check in with five people (my Fab Five, as I thought of them) by 6:00 p.m. each night. Some nights, it was just a simple text to let them know I was okay. Once or twice, when I knew I was settled into a location for a few days, I let them know when I got to town and when I would be leaving, but I didn't necessarily text every day during the stay.

On day forty, I arrived in Columbia Falls, Montana, where I was excited to stay for a few nights and visit Glacier National Park. I let the Fab Five know I had reached town, and I headed to the park. The wind was whipping at Lake McDonald, and the temperature was in the single digits. Many roads were blocked because of the snow. I sent photos and videos to the Fab Five that night, telling them how cold it was.

The next morning, I asked the hotel clerk for a recommendation for a good sightseeing area. He told me about a town called Polebridge and gave me directions. I set off around 11:00 a.m. The road from Glacier Falls to Polebridge is mostly dirt, and after about five miles, there is no cell signal. It didn't matter to me; I had been on many such roads, and it was a cold but beautiful day. I was really hoping to find some moose in the area to photograph.

About twenty miles in, I passed an education center that appeared to be deserted and saw a sign for Moose Lake Road. *Hey,* I thought to myself, *I should go there instead because there might actually be moose at Moose Lake!* I turned left and went where the road took me. The road was extremely rough with potholes, but there were no signs indicating it was closed (as there had been in many areas at Glacier Park). So, I kept going, albeit slowly. I drove five miles before I saw the first bit of snow on the ground. Nothing to worry about—it wasn't deep at all, and the sun was still out. After another three miles, my gut started telling me to turn around, but I didn't listen. I justified it by telling myself there wasn't enough room to turn around, but at that point I could have easily backed up. Plus, I *really* wanted to find a moose! Two miles beyond that, I crossed a narrow bridge and had a decision to make. To my left was a wide-open space to turn around; ahead was an incline, and the snow had become very deep. I finally listened to that still, small voice and turned around. Following my tracks, the only ones in the snow, I crossed the bridge again and drove 500 feet up the road before my left rear tire got stuck. The spot was just a bit deeper than the other tracks I had created, but I didn't realize it until it was too late. Again, nothing to worry about—I had been stuck in the snow before, so I calmly got out and started to dig. I placed branches under my tires. I removed tires to put on chains because it's not as easy as the directions make it appear. And yes, I should have put those chains on before I drove in the snow. Hindsight, and all that . . .

I never panicked, but I was annoyed with myself for not trusting my instinct sooner, and I was cold—it was about twenty-five degrees. Five hours later, despite trying everything I could think of, I was soaking wet and still stuck, and I knew I couldn't hike out before it got dark. I got back in the Voyager and hunkered down until help arrived. After all, the Fab Five would send someone to look for me, right?

Lesson Eight: It's not just about me; we are all connected.

Although everyone's journey is unique, most people will experience grief due to loss at some point in their lives. There are billions of people, at any given time, grieving something or someone, but when we're in the thick of it, we feel like no one understands what we are going through. This can create a "me against the world" mentality and may stall the healing process by causing us to isolate or avoid seeking help. With time, we find others who share a similar story or are grieving in much the same way, which reminds us we are not alone.

As I said earlier, when Pam was alive, I felt like it was my job to keep her safe. Since Pam died, I thought I didn't have to be as careful because I didn't have to be safe for her anymore. Even though I have family and friends who love me, for the past twenty months, and especially on this road trip, I hadn't really been considering the consequences of all my actions. If I had, I most certainly would not have gone down Moose Lake Road.

It's deeper than it looks!

I gave up all thoughts of rescue sometime around midnight. I was never afraid, although if this had happened at the beginning of my trip, I probably would have been. I tried to sleep in my car, but all I could think about was how worried my mom must be. Although I was also concerned about my son, dad, brother, and friends, it made me sick to my stomach to think what my actions were doing to my mom since I knew how frantic I would be if my son was missing. It was a very long night full of much contemplation. I tried to send a message mentally to one of my best friends (part of the Fab Five). Throughout the night, I kept repeating, "I'm stuck in the snow on Moose Lake Road; send help . . . but I'm okay!" By the next morning, I was exhausted and deeply humbled. I was also very anxious to get a phone signal so I could let my family know I was okay.

This experience made me realize deep down that there are still some people I want to stay safe for—not because they rely on me the same way Pam did, but because they would be in pain if something happened to me. I already knew that intellectually, but I truly felt it on an emotional level on that long, cold night.

Here is where I listened to my intuition; I wanted to leave the car at first light, but something told me to stay put. This time, I didn't argue. I waited until 7:30 a.m., and when it felt "right," I set out with the backpack full of emergency supplies that my twin brother had given me for the trip, which later became crucial. Dressed in two pairs of snow pants, a snow jacket, and hiking boots, I carried a walking stick in one hand and a can of bear spray in the other. I came across several animal tracks during the hike out, all of which appeared to be very fresh; they were there on top of the tire tracks that I had left the day before. Some were cat tracks, and while I didn't know at that time which type of cat had left those marks, I later learned that there are mountain lions in that area, in addition to bears and moose. Seeing all those tracks made me grateful I hadn't ventured out sooner.

The adrenaline and the need to call my people kept me going, but I could tell I was getting dehydrated; I was extremely fatigued and starting to get dizzy. The water bottle on the outside of my backpack froze while I was walking. Luckily, there were pouches of water inside the backpack, so I took a quick break and washed a granola bar down with water. I said a silent "thank you" to my brother, who has looked out for me since we were kids. I wanted nothing more than to lie down and rest, but I had to keep going. Every half mile, I stopped and yelled, "Hello!" hoping that someone would answer. All that returned from the vast emptiness to my right was the echo of my own tired voice.

About seven miles up the road, I saw three pickup trucks way off in the distance coming toward me. At first, I thought I was hallucinating. When I realized I wasn't, a wave of relief washed over me. I was overwhelmed with emotion and almost cried, except my tears would have likely frozen before they hit my cheeks. The trucks suddenly stopped, and I worried that they were going to leave. I frantically waved my arms back and forth. I was so exhausted that I could barely move, but I had to get to them before they left. I used my last bit of strength to catch up to them and found three men hauling snowmobiles trying to find a place to ride. After I told them my story, they laughed and said that when they saw me, they initially thought I was an animal. When they realized I was a person, they figured I was either in need of help or something shady was going on. No wonder they stopped in their tracks! One of them gave me a ride three miles down the road to the education center, which was now occupied by several staff and parents dropping their kids off for a field trip. A kind staff member brought me hot tea and a granola bar. The man who took me to the center secured me another ride for the remaining miles to my hotel. Before we left, I used the Wi-Fi at the center and called my son. When he picked up, he said casually and cheerfully, "Hey Mom! How ya doing?"

Through no fault of their own and solely due to my lack of communication, four of the Fab Five didn't even realize I was missing. The friend I sent the mental message to seemed to have received part of it, at least. I had several text messages from her asking where I was, and she later told me she thought I might be stuck in the snow, but she also knew I was okay. I was so grateful that my friends and family weren't worried about me all night, and I vowed to never do anything like that again. I called my parents and told them about my adventure once I was safely back in my hotel room.

The next day, I rode out with a tow crew to retrieve my car, but the tow truck itself got stuck in the snow several miles from my car. It took five hours to pull the truck out of the snow, and my car remained unretrieved for one more night. The following day, another tow driver came in (on his day off), picked me up at my hotel, and drove to Moose Lake Road. I ran into the same three snowmobilers when we were five miles from my car. One of them offered to give me a ride on his snowmobile to my car, and of course I said yes! The tow driver met me at my car and was able to free it; I drove the rest of the way.

Here is where lessons two and four were reinforced. There were so many great people who helped me during this adventure. The snowmobilers, the staff at the education center, the woman who drove me back to my hotel, the tow truck drivers—especially the one who came in on his day off. The snowmobilers even texted me later to make sure I was okay. I realized that people are better than I thought they were, and I had allowed myself to trust the ones who came to my aid.

Lessons seven and eight reminded me to follow my instincts and that we are all connected. My actions can have a positive or negative effect on those around me, both near and far. I'm so grateful that my friends and family didn't worry about me that night, but on the other hand, I'm glad I was concerned about them all night because this was the best lesson I learned on my journey.

I made an appointment to get my car checked to make sure it was safe to drive. I wasn't taking any more chances! This gave me a few days to hang out in the hotel and ponder over the lessons learned on this trip. I knew there was at least one more I really needed to work on…

Week 7

Lesson Nine: Forgiveness is essential for healing.

Tremendous guilt seems to be one of the top ten issues for widows and widowers, or for anyone grieving a loss. No matter how good the relationship was, guilt has a way of creeping in. My primary source of guilt was not being there with Pam when she died, even though I had been with her just hours before. I also felt a lot of guilt for not getting her to the hospital sooner. You can probably include anger in that top ten list too. Anger at the person for dying and at yourself for not doing things differently. There is anger at friends, family, and even strangers who say or do the wrong things, and anger about legal and financial matters that come up later.

I thought I had already processed most of the guilt and anger, but in early 2022, it seemed it was back again. As the weeks rolled by on the road trip, I felt that pent-up guilt and anger start to subside. This journey was reducing my stress and helping me see what was important. Hanging on to guilt and anger would create nothing positive, and in fact, doing so was preventing me from healing and living my best life. I can never change the fact that Pam has died, but I can try to have a positive attitude as I move forward. Occasionally, negative feelings still present themselves, but it helps to think back to my time on the road and to remember what is important: love, forgiveness, patience, compassion—for others and for myself.

My car was inspected and given a clean bill of health. I promised my family and friends that I would be extra careful on the rest of the journey, so I decided on a safe visit to a museum in Kalispell, Montana. It was a nice change of pace, and I learned a lot about the history of that town.

From Kalispell, I headed to Wallace, Idaho—my first time in that state. I photographed Hecla Mine, an old silver mine in Burke, Idaho, and took time to reflect on what life in that area must have been like in the late 1800s, when the town was in full swing.

As week seven ended, I crossed the state line from Idaho to Washington—back home! The Palouse Scenic Byway is one of the most beautiful and most photographed places in the state. I checked into my hotel in Colfax, headed out to Kamiak Butte County Park, then took the long, winding drive up to Steptoe Butte State Park just before sunset. My trip would soon come to an end, and I was determined to make the most of my last few days on the road.

Week 8

The next day, I took a long drive to Palouse Falls State Park, then went to Boyer Park and Marina and the Lower Granite Dam. I found several abandoned and broken-down buildings along the way. Before I left Colfax, I drove to the wind turbines. They are a sight to see from a distance, and they're even more incredible up close!

I made a quick stop at Govan Ghost Town to snap photos of the old 1905 schoolhouse.

My last stop before home was the Bavarian town of Leavenworth—one of my favorites ever since I was a little kid. It somehow felt right to spend my last three nights there. Day fifty-three started with an early morning horseback ride before an afternoon drive. Washington State is known for its apples, and being early in the season, I was able to get photos of the trees in bloom—thousands upon thousands of them! Evenings were spent in the hotel lobby with other guests, listening to live piano music. This was pure relaxation and one of the things I enjoyed the most in Leavenworth.

On day fifty-five, I packed up slowly and headed west over Stevens Pass in the Cascade Range. I stopped at the river on the way home to listen to the rush of the water and mentally prepare myself for going home. In contrast to how I felt after the fourth week, going home now felt okay, and I was excited to see family and friends again. I was amazed at how different I was from just eight weeks prior. I was more confident and secure, no longer afraid, and I felt good about myself—really good—for perhaps the first time since Pam's death.

I knew how much of an impact this journey had on me, but I couldn't really articulate it until I started writing this book. About midway through writing, lesson ten surfaced, which helped me put it into words . . .

Lesson Ten: Grief comes with an emergency exit.

In a smoke-filled building, it's hard to find your way out. The smoke causes pain and tightness in your chest and makes it hard to breathe. Your eyes water, your sense of time distorts, and you may feel like you're going to die. Anyone who has grieved the death of a loved one has probably felt this same way.

Like most buildings, grief has an emergency exit. If you persevere, you can get through the absolute misery and pain and come out on the other side. It doesn't mean you will ever stop loving the one who died, and it doesn't even mean you will stop grieving or being sad about their death. But you can find a way to survive and learn to live with, and even embrace, your new reality.

Your emergency exit doesn't have to be a road trip. It can be anything that helps to reset your brain and shake up your grief. Find something you love or are passionate about, and allow yourself to be fully immersed in it. Try to have healthy new experiences and allow new people into your life if that helps you on your journey. You are worthy of self-care.

The Solo Becky Project was my emergency exit. Some friends and strangers describe my trip as exciting and call me brave or adventurous. Yes, the trip was exciting, and at times maybe I was brave or adventurous (or a little reckless), but it didn't necessarily feel like that at the time; all I knew for certain was that this trip was essential for my mental health, and I can't imagine the emotional state that I would be in today if I hadn't made myself a priority and taken that journey.

All told, I drove 7,284 miles in those fifty-five days on the road. When I left, I had no idea what I was looking for. Somewhere along the way, I found myself.